The Spirit of Buddha

The Spirit of Buddha

Photographs by Robin Kyte-Coles

Foreword by His Holiness the Dalai Lama

teNeues

THE DALAI LAMA

Foreword by His Holiness the Dalai Lama

Shakyamuni Buddha attained enlightenment and taught in India over two thousand years ago, yet his teaching remains refreshing and relevant today. This is because no matter who we are or where we live, we all want happiness and dislike suffering.

I am often asked whether the teaching and practice of Buddhism, with its origins in ancient India, are suitable for people living in our modern world. I believe they are, because, like all religions, Buddhism deals with basic human problems. Therefore, as long as we continue to experience the basic human sufferings of birth, disease, old age, and death, there is no question as to whether the Buddha's advice is suitable or not. And I do not believe that you have to be a Buddhist to benefit from it. The key is inner peace. If we have that, we can face difficulties with calm and reason while keeping our inner happiness intact. The Buddha's teachings of love, kindness and tolerance, the conduct of nonviolence, and especially the theory that all things are relative can be a source of that inner peace.

In the Buddhist tradition we remember the Buddha as a great teacher who showed the path to ultimate peace and happiness for all sentient beings. Statues and paintings remind us of his physical presence, the scriptures contain a record of his speech and the advice he gave, while *stupas* represent the Buddha's mind, which is essentially at peace.

The image of the Buddha represents not only the historical Buddha, Shakyamuni, but also the ultimate state of enlightenment we all can achieve. His depiction in the posture of meditation reminds us of the importance of meditation on the path to enlightenment. The serene expression on his face reveals that he achieved the bliss of enlightenment by the nonviolent means of purifying the mind of all obstacles and accomplishing all qualities. His only weapons were love, compassion and wisdom.

Many of Robin Kyte-Coles' photographs of Buddhist images presented in this fine book convey such qualities. I hope that as readers go through the book they will remember the Buddha's essential message of nonviolence, that we should try to help others as much as we can, and that even if we cannot actually be of help, we should at least be careful not to do anyone harm.

Vorwort von Seiner Heiligkeit dem Dalai Lama

Die Lehre Shakyamuni Buddhas, der vor über zweitausend Jahren in Indien zur Erleuchtung gelangte, ist auch heute noch lebendig und von Bedeutung, da wir alle, gleich wer wir sind und wo wir leben, nach Glück streben und Leid zu vermeiden suchen.

Ich werde oft gefragt, ob die Lehre und Praxis des Buddhismus, dessen Ursprünge im alten Indien liegen, eine Bedeutung für Menschen haben, die in unserer modernen Welt leben. Ich glaube, dass sie uns etwas angehen, weil sich der Buddhismus wie alle Religionen mit den Grundproblemen der Menschen befasst. Daher steht es außer Frage, dass uns die Lehre Buddhas noch betrifft, solange Geburt, Krankheit, Alter und Tod zu den leidvollen menschlichen Erfahrungen gehören. Ich glaube, man muss nicht Buddhist sein, um Gewinn aus der Lehre des Buddhismus zu ziehen. Der Schlüssel ist der innere Frieden. Wenn wir diesen gefunden haben, können wir Schwierigkeiten mit Ruhe und Vernunft meistern und gleichzeitig unser inneres Glück bewahren. Buddhas Lehre, die auf Liebe, Güte und Toleranz, Verzicht auf Gewalt in unserem Verhalten und besonders auf der Theorie beruht, dass alle Dinge nur relative Bedeutung haben, kann zur Quelle dieses inneren Friedens werden.

In der buddhistischen Tradition gedenken wir Buddhas als eines großen Lehrers, der allen fühlenden Wesen den Weg zu höchstem Frieden und Glück gezeigt hat. Statuen und Bilder erinnern uns an seine physische Erscheinung, die Schriften enthalten die Aufzeichnung seiner Reden und Lehren. Die *Stupas* schließlich verkörpern Buddhas Geist, ruhend in wahrhaftigem Frieden.

Die Darstellungen Buddhas zeigen nicht nur den historischen Buddha, Shakyamuni, sondern auch die höchste Stufe der Erleuchtung, die wir alle erreichen können. Seine Abbildung in der Haltung der Meditation erinnert uns an die Bedeutung der Meditation auf dem Weg zur Erleuchtung. Sein gelassen heiterer Gesichtsausdruck offenbart, dass er die Seligkeit der Erleuchtung erlangt hat, indem er auf gewaltlose Weise seinen Geist von allen Hindernissen befreit und alle Fähigkeiten vervollkommnet hat. Seine einzigen Waffen waren Liebe, Mitgefühl und Weisheit.

Viele der Fotografien von Robin Kyte-Coles mit Darstellungen Buddhas, die in diesem schönen Band vereint sind, vermitteln diese Eigenschaften. Ich hoffe, dass uns Buddhas zentrale Botschaft der Gewaltlosigkeit beim Ansehen des Buches bewusst wird und uns inspiriert, anderen nach Kräften zu helfen und, wenn wir im Augenblick nicht helfen können, zumindest darauf zu achten, niemandem Schaden zuzufügen.

Préface de Sa Sainteté le Dalaï-Lama

Sakyamuni Bouddha atteignit l'illumination et enseigna en Inde voici plus de deux mille ans, mais sa doctrine est toujours vivante et pertinente. En effet, qui que nous soyons et où que nous vivions, nous recherchons tous le bonheur et rejetons la souffrance.

On me demande souvent si l'enseignement et la pratique du bouddhisme, qui a ses racines dans l'Inde antique, sont adaptés à notre monde moderne. Je pense que oui, car, comme toutes les religions, le bouddhisme aborde les problèmes humains essentiels. C'est pourquoi, tant que nous éprouverons les souffrances humaines fondamentales de la naissance, de la maladie, de la vieillesse et de la mort, les conseils du Bouddha seront appropriés. Et je ne pense pas qu'il soit nécessaire d'être bouddhiste pour en profiter. La clé est la paix intérieure. Celui qui la possède peut affronter les difficultés avec calme et raison, tout en gardant intact son bonheur intérieur. Les enseignements du Bouddha sur l'amour, la bonté et la tolérance, la pratique de la non-violence et, en particulier, la relativité de toutes choses, peuvent conduire à cette paix intérieure.

Dans la tradition bouddhiste, nous nous souvenons du Bouddha comme d'un grand maître qui a montré le chemin vers la paix ultime et le bonheur pour tous les êtres sensibles. Les statues et les peintures rappellent sa présence physique, les écritures ont consigné sa parole et ses conseils, tandis que les *stupas* symbolisent son esprit, qui est essentiellement en paix.

L'image du Bouddha évoque non seulement le Bouddha historique, Sakyamuni, mais aussi le stade ultime d'Éveil auquel nous pouvons tous parvenir. Sa représentation en posture de méditation nous rappelle l'importance de celle-ci sur le chemin d'illumination. L'expression sereine de son visage révèle qu'il a atteint la félicité de l'Éveil par des moyens non-violents : la purification de l'esprit de tous les obstacles, et l'accomplissement de toutes les qualités. L'amour, la compassion et la sagesse.

Dans ce beau livre, de nombreuses photographies d'images bouddhiques réalisées par Robin Kyte-Coles évoquent ces qualités. J'espère qu'en le feuilletant, les lecteurs se souviendront que Bouddha a prôné la non-violence et l'entraide, et que s'il nous est impossible d'offrir notre aide, de veiller au moins à ne pas faire de mal à qui que ce soit.

Prólogo de Su Santidad el Dalai Lama

Shakyamuni Buda alcanzó la iluminación y prodigó sus enseñanzas en la India hace más de dos mil años, pero sus doctrinas siguen siendo actuales y relevantes aún en nuestros días. La razón es que, independientemente de quiénes seamos o dónde vivamos, todos buscamos la felicidad y rechazamos el sufrimiento.

Me han preguntado muchas veces si la enseñanza y la práctica del budismo, surgido en la antigua India, son compatibles con la vida moderna. Yo así lo creo porque, como todas las religiones, el budismo se ocupa de los problemas humanos básicos. Por eso, mientras sigamos experimentando el dolor existencial del nacimiento, la enfermedad, el envejecimiento y la muerte, es indudable que las enseñanzas del Buda seguirán gozando de plena actualidad. Y no creo que haya que ser budista para beneficiarse de ellas. La clave es la paz interior. Si estamos en paz seremos capaces de enfrentar las dificultades con calma y racionalidad, y nuestra felicidad interna quedará intacta. Las enseñanzas del Buda sobre el amor, la bondad y la tolerancia, la actitud de no violencia y especialmente la teoría de que todas las cosas son relativas pueden ser una fuente de paz interior.

En la tradición budista recordamos al Buda como un gran maestro que mostró el camino de la paz y la felicidad definitivas a todos los seres conscientes. Estatuas y pinturas nos recuerdan su presencia física, las escrituras contienen la memoria de sus enseñanzas y recomendaciones, y las *estupas* representan su mente, esencialmente en paz.

Hoy en día, la imagen del Buda no sólo representa al personaje histórico, Shakyamuni, sino que simboliza el máximo estado de iluminación que todos podemos alcanzar. Su descripción en la postura meditativa nos recuerda la importancia de la meditación como camino hacia la sabiduría. La serena expresión de su rostro revela que alcanzó la felicidad de la iluminación por los medios no violentos de purificar la mente de cualquier obstáculo y cultivar todas las cualidades. Sus únicas armas eran el amor, la compasión y la sabiduría.

Muchas de las imágenes budistas de Robin Kyte-Coles que se presentan en esta excelente obra reúnen esas cualidades. Espero que todos aquellos que lean el libro recuerden el mensaje esencial de no violencia del Buda: debemos tratar siempre de ayudar a los demás y, cuando tal cosa no sea posible, por lo menos evitar hacer daño a nadie.

Prefazione di Sua Santità il Dalai Lama

Shakyamuni Buddha raggiunse l'illuminazione e insegnò in India oltre duemila anni fa, eppure il suo insegnamento è ancora oggi un'importante fonte di sostegno morale, dal momento che tutti noi – chiunque siamo o dovunque viviamo – inseguiamo la felicità e rifuggiamo le sofferenze.

Spesso mi viene chiesto se l'insegnamento e la pratica del buddismo, con le sue origini che affondano nell'antica India, siano ancora validi per l'uomo contemporaneo. Sono convinto che lo siano perché, come tutte le religioni, il buddismo risponde ai problemi fondamentali delle persone. Per questo, fintanto che continuiamo a provare le esperienze di sofferenza che accomunano tutti gli esseri umani nel corso della loro esistenza, quali la nascita, la malattia, la vecchiaia e la morte, non vi è alcun dubbio che i consigli del Buddha siano ancora attuali, né ritengo che sia necessario essere buddisti per trarne beneficio. La chiave è la pace interiore; se la possediamo siamo in grado di affrontare le difficoltà con calma e ragionevolezza, mantenendo intatta la nostra felicità spirituale. Gli insegnamenti del Buddha sull'amore, sulla gentilezza e sulla tolleranza, la pratica della non violenza e in particolare la teoria secondo la quale tutte le cose sono relative, possono costituire una fonte di questa pace.

Nella tradizione buddhista ricordiamo il Buddha come un grande maestro che ha indicato la via per la pace e la felicità suprema per tutti gli esseri animati. Le statue e i dipinti ci ricordano la sua presenza fisica, le scritture contengono un resoconto delle sue parole e dei consigli che diede ai suoi seguaci, mentre gli *stupa* rappresentano la mente del Buddha nel raggiungimento della pace suprema.

L'immagine del Buddha non rappresenta solamente il Buddha storico, Shakyamuni, ma anche lo stato supremo di illuminazione che ognuno di noi può raggiungere. La posizione di meditazione in cui è rappresentato vuole ricordarci l'importanza che questa occupa sulla via che porta all'illuminazione. L'espressione serena del suo volto ci ricorda che egli raggiunse la beatitudine dell'illuminazione con il mezzo non violento della purificazione della mente da tutti gli ostacoli e il perfezionamento di ogni qualità personale. Le sue uniche armi erano l'amore, la compassione e la saggezza.

Molte delle fotografie di immagini buddiste realizzate da Robin Kyte-Coles e presentate in questo magnifico volume esprimono tali qualità. Spero che, addentrandosi in questo libro, i lettori ricordino il messaggio fondamentale del Buddha, ovvero la non violenza come invito ad aiutare il prossimo oppure, ove questo non sia possibile, quantomeno a non nuocergli.

Wisdom and Compassion Expressed Through the Arts

Around 2,500 years ago, a boy called Siddhartha was born into a royal family in a kingdom covering parts of what are now northern India and southern Nepal. He was born into a royal life of luxury and he possessed many worldly pleasurable things such as palaces, beautiful objects, great wealth, elephants, horses, servants and so forth. He also participated in all sorts of royal pleasurable activities. He was married and had a son, but by around the age of 27 this man called Siddhartha was very much searching for the truth about the nature of life. It was then that, following the custom of the day, he renounced worldly life and devoted himself to the search for that truth. He left the security of his palaces, his wife and son, and all the pleasurable things and activities behind and went off to search for the truth of the nature of life. For a long time he searched for an answer to this question, joining many wise teachers of his day and studying their answers to the question of what is the nature of this life. He practiced many meditations and great austerities, until finally realizing that austerity and asceticism by themselves were not a way to discover the meaning he was searching for. Eventually he famously went and sat under the Bodhi tree and vowed not to move until his quest was fulfilled. It was there that his search reached its final result and he found the answer to his quest. That answer was no mere intellectual understanding but a process that had led him to becoming fully awakened to the nature of reality including the nature of this life. It was because of this great realization that he was called the Buddha. The "Buddha" in Sanskrit literally means the awakened one. Here, to be awakened means that his mind was fully awakened in the form of great compassion and wisdom—a wisdom about the true nature of reality and a compassion that encompasses all living beings. It is these qualities that are referred to here in the word Buddha—to be awakened. Through this awakened mind, the Buddha gave teachings for almost 45 to 46 years until his death. His teachings were mainly given to cultivate within each and every living being compassion and wisdom according to their capacities. That kind of compassion and even wisdom are very common practices in all the world's religions.

In Buddhism, its uniqueness is that these practices are undertaken without believing in an eternal supernatural being, without asserting a creator, but simply acknowledging each and every living being possesses the potential for himself or herself to become a fully awakened being if he or she cultivates compassion and wisdom. The essence of this practice of compassion is to start with nonviolence which is one of the most essential teachings the Buddha has given to us. Here, nonviolence does not mean only to avoid physical and verbal violence or destroying the peace and happiness of other people and other beings. Here, practicing nonviolence is mainly focused on dealing with internal violence. The focus is to understand and counter what in Buddhism are called the three poisons—attachment, aversion and ignorance. These three are the source from which comes the impulse for external physical and verbal violence. So in Buddhism the belief is that external violence comes from internal violence and until we learn to deal with internal violence, such as attachment, aversion and ignorance, then merely avoiding external violence will not be that fruitful and will not bring long-lasting peace. Therefore, in Buddhism, practicing compassion is very much dealing with these unhealthy internal mental states. The root of these states is seen as a fundamental misunderstanding of the nature of ourselves and other phenomena. It is from this ignorance that attachment and aversion and all the consequential negative emotions arise. The key to deal with this fundamental ignorance is the development of wisdom, from a basic equanimity right up to a full understanding of the subtlest modes of our existence. These unhealthy or distorted mental states such as attachment, aversion and ignorance and their associated negative emotions arise naturally without wisdom. Wisdom here refers to seeing things and events such as they really are without exaggeration and without unnecessary expectations. Cultivating this way of seeing things and events as they really are is the most important understanding to be developed in the context of wisdom and it is the most important quality to cultivate to counteract internal violence. Therefore, combining compassion and wisdom is key. It is the development of compassion in the sense of initially reducing, then tackling and eliminating internal violence through the cultivation of wisdom. This is called the union of wisdom and compassion and that is the core message and the core teaching that the Buddha gave to his followers.

The many Buddhist arts express very clearly these two qualities, wisdom and compassion, through their manifestations in works such as in sculpture and in the development of *stupas*. Buddhist art objects are not objects of worship but are produced mainly to raise awareness in each and every human being of our innermost potential to become a fully awakened being, to become free from ignorance and to achieve illumination. These art objects express the journey from ignorance to illumination. Although there is a lot of debate by historians whether there were or were not statues of the Buddha in his lifetime, there is no doubt that in the

Buddha's time in India there were many great religious traditions such as Brahmanism and Jainism and other major spiritual traditions with well-developed arts. All spiritual traditions celebrate their special festivals and events through great buildings or other arts. Like all spiritual traditions, Buddhism has its own special events to commemorate or to celebrate. Some of the earliest Buddhist art works were the monuments that over the years have developed into the art form of the *stupa*. It seems that soon after the Buddha passed away, his followers built a monument at the place where the Buddha was cremated in Kushinagar, located in northern India. This was perhaps the earliest Buddhist *stupa*, a solid mound that gradually became surrounded by other structures. As was the tradition of the day, when the ashes of the Buddha were divided amongst some of his closest disciples and the kings of that area, then it was natural for them to build *stupas*. These *stupas* kept the Buddha's ashes in a safe place where the public could come to pay their respects and to venerate the Buddha. Originally, these were very much just big, solid mounds in a variety of sizes constructed of bricks or simply made from a huge amount of earth. In the middle or in the center lies a metal, stone or clay box where the ashes were placed and around that the structure was built. Later on, different shapes and structures evolved and a rich variety of styles of *stupas* arose when Buddhism spread towards the south and east in Sri Lanka, Burma, Thailand and Indonesia, and also to the north and west in Kashmir, Afghanistan, Nepal, Tibet and as far as China and Japan. Nowadays, we can see many different kinds of *stupas* in these countries and a vibrant tradition of using them for religious purposes still flourishes in all Buddhist countries and places. Another Buddhist art is drawing and sculpting images of the Buddha. It is said that in the early days of Buddhism, maybe for the first few hundred years, there were no images of the Buddha. In order to commemorate and to remember the Buddha and his teachings, the images used were the Bodhi tree, the wheel representing the Buddha *dharma*, the footprint of the Buddha, or the deeply symbolic lotus and so forth. It is later that images of the Buddha came into being.

The geographic spread of Buddhism and the development of Buddhist thought produced different traditions sometimes called Southern and Northern traditions, or sometimes called the Theravada, the earliest or elder Buddhist tradition, and the Mahayana tradition. These different traditions of Buddhism have naturally come to have different interpretations of Buddhist imagery and many styles evolved within these traditions. In the earliest representations of the Buddha image, the Buddha statues were built from rock, wood or clay. Later they were built from metals, bronze, silver as well as gold. The differing traditions with their statues in different sizes and styles share one thing in common: the images produced are not supposed to be accurate representations of the Buddha; they do not show how he actually looked during his life. Commonly, all these images are used to express his teachings, and of course this means his teachings on compassion and wisdom. One surprising fact when we look at all these statues produced across millennia and separated by vast distances is the great similarity in basic postures and gestures. The different traditions and styles also share a common expression in the representation of the face of Buddha. His eyes are open in a very gentle gaze to express his compassion, his right hand is touching the earth to demonstrate that he has overcome the delusions, attachments, aversions, ignorance and so forth. He is often seated in a meditative pose. That kind of expression and posture is shared in common. All these representations are there to demonstrate and to deepen our understanding of his teachings on compassion and wisdom and to remind us that we too can cultivate that kind of awakening mind within ourselves. The representations of the Buddha show him sitting, standing, walking, and with different hand gestures. All these bodily expressions are very much spontaneous expressions to explain that each and every living being possesses the potential to have compassion and wisdom. Just like modern psychology has developed a science of body language that explains through the postures of a person what is happening mentally inside them, so too is it the same in these different hand gestures, and activities of walking, sitting and lying down. They are all the spontaneous natural expressions of inner pristine awareness of wisdom and compassion. Each of these gestures has a different meaning and these gestures are not contrived artificial expressions, they are all spontaneous natural expressions that have a deep appeal to us even across cultural boundaries. Hopefully a study of these Buddhist arts will strike a resonant note deep within the reader, a note that will vibrate in sympathy with the natural spontaneous expressions of compassion and wisdom within all of us.

Geshe Tashi Tsering,
Tibetan Buddhist Monk,
resident teacher at Jamyang Buddhist Centre

Ausdruck von Weisheit und Mitgefühl in der Kunst

Vor 2500 Jahren kam ein Knabe mit Namen Siddhartha in einer königlichen Familie zur Welt, deren Reich sich über einen Teil des Gebiets des heutigen Nordindien und Südnepal erstreckte. Er führte ein königliches Leben voller Luxus und besaß viele Dinge, die zu den Annehmlichkeiten eines weltlichen Daseins gehörten: ein großes Vermögen, kostbare Gegenstände, Paläste, Elefanten, Pferde und Diener. Er genoss die Freuden des königlichen Lebens, war verheiratet und hatte einen Sohn. Im Alter von ungefähr 27 Jahren jedoch machte sich Siddhartha auf die intensive Suche nach der Wahrheit über die Natur unseres Daseins. Er entsagte, einem Brauch der Zeit folgend, dem weltlichen Leben und widmete sich dieser Suche. Dafür verzichtete er auf das gesicherte Leben im Palast, verließ seine Frau und seinen Sohn, gab alle Vergnügungen und Tätigkeiten auf und ging fort. Auf der langen Suche nach einer Antwort wandte er sich an viele weise Lehrer der damaligen Zeit und studierte ihre Erkenntnisse über die Natur des Lebens. Er widmete sich der Meditation und großer Entsagung, bis er schließlich erkannte, dass Entsagung und Askese nicht der richtige Weg zur Erkenntnis des Sinns waren, nach dem er suchte. Schließlich setzte er sich unter den Bodhi-Baum und gelobte, dort so lange zu verharren, bis sein Streben sich erfüllte. Dort fand ein Erlebnis statt, das seine Suche zu einem endgültigen Ergebnis führte und ihm die Antwort auf seine Frage gab. Die Antwort bestand nicht in einer intellektuellen Erkenntnis, sondern in einem Prozess, der ihn zu vollem Erwachen und zur Erkenntnis der Natur der Wirklichkeit und auch der seines eigenen Lebens führte. Wegen dieser großen Erkenntnis wurde er Buddha genannt. „Buddha" bedeutet im Sanskrit wörtlich „der Erwachte". In diesem Fall bedeutet „erwacht", dass sein Geist vollständig erwacht und von großem Mitgefühl und Weisheit erfüllt war – Weisheit über das wahre Wesen der Wirklichkeit und Mitgefühl, das alle Lebewesen umfasst. Alle diese hier erwähnten Eigenschaften drückt das Wort „Buddha" aus – erwacht sein. Als Erwachter lehrte Buddha 45 oder 46 Jahre bis zu seinem Tod. Seine Lehrtätigkeit richtete sich vor allem darauf, in jedem Lebewesen Mitgefühl und Weisheit je nach seinen Fähigkeiten zu entwickeln. Diese Art von Mitgefühl und jede Art von Weisheit sind bekannte Praktiken in allen Weltreligionen.

Das Einzigartige des Buddhismus liegt darin, dass alle diese Praktiken angewandt werden ohne den Glauben an ein ewiges oder übernatürliches Wesen, ohne die Behauptung der Existenz eines Schöpfers, allein dadurch, dass jedem Wesen die Fähigkeit zuerkannt wird, ein vollständig erwachtes Wesen zu werden, wenn es Mitgefühl und Weisheit entwickelt. Der Kern dieser Praxis des Mitgefühls liegt zunächst darin, Gewaltlosigkeit zu üben, die zu den wesentlichsten Lehren gehört, die Buddha uns vermittelt hat. Gewaltlosigkeit bedeutet in diesem Fall nicht nur, physische oder verbale Gewalt zu meiden oder Frieden und Glück anderer Menschen oder anderer Wesen nicht zu zerstören. Die Praxis der Gewaltlosigkeit ist vor allem auf die innere Gewalttätigkeit gerichtet. Dieser Fokus soll Erkenntnis und Widerstand gegen die im Buddhismus so genannten drei Gifte wecken – Begehren, Abneigung und Unwissenheit. Diese drei sind die Quelle, aus der sich der Impuls zu physischer und verbaler Gewalt speist. So beruht der Buddhismus auf dem Glauben, dass äußere Gewalt durch innere Gewalt erzeugt wird. Solange wir nicht gelernt haben, mit der inneren Gewalt fertig zu werden, wird auch das Vermeiden äußerer Gewalt nicht wirklich fruchtbar sein und zu keinem dauerhaften Frieden führen. Daher hat die Praxis des Mitgefühls im Buddhismus viel damit zu tun, ungesunde innere Einstellungen zu überwinden. Als Wurzel dieser Einstellungen wird die grundlegende Unkenntnis über unsere eigene Natur und die anderer Erscheinungen betrachtet. Daraus entstehen Begehren, Abneigung und alle daraus folgenden negativen Gefühle. Der Schlüssel zur Bekämpfung dieser fundamentalen Unwissenheit ist die Erlangung von Weisheit, die aus Gelassenheit entspringt und zum vollständigen Verständnis auch der schlichtesten Formen der Existenz führt. Derart ungesunde und fehlgeleitete Geisteszustände wie Begehren, Abneigung und Unwissenheit und die damit verbundenen negativen Gefühle entspringen natürlich einem Mangel an Weisheit. Weisheit erlaubt Dinge und Ereignisse so zu sehen, wie sie wirklich sind, ohne Übertreibungen und ohne unnötige Erwartungen. Die Dinge so zu sehen, wie sie wirklich sind, ist von größter Wichtigkeit bei der Erlangung von Weisheit und stellt die wichtigste Eigenschaft dar, die benötigt wird, um der inneren Gewalt entgegenzuwirken. Daher bildet die Verbindung von Mitgefühl und Weisheit den Schlüssel. Darunter ist die Entstehung von Mitgefühl im Sinn von anfänglicher Verringerung, darauf folgender Bekämpfung und schließlich Eliminierung von innerer Gewalt durch die Entwicklung von Weisheit zu verstehen. Das wird als Einheit von Weisheit und Mitgefühl bezeichnet, und darin besteht der Kern der Botschaft, die der Buddha seinen Nachfolgern mitgegeben hat.

Die zahlreichen buddhistischen Kunstwerke bringen diese beiden Eigenschaften, Weisheit und Mitgefühl, sehr klar zum Ausdruck, in Form von Werken wie Skulpturen und durch die Gestaltung von *Stupas*. Buddhistische Kunstobjekte sind nicht zur Anbetung bestimmt, sondern sollen in jedem menschlichen Wesen zum Erwachen beitragen, indem sie das uns innewohnende Potential aktivieren, zu einem vollständig erwachten Lebewesen zu werden, uns von Unwissenheit zu befreien und die Erleuchtung zu vollenden. Diese

Kunstobjekte veranschaulichen den Weg von der Unwissenheit zur Erleuchtung. Obwohl es unter den Historikern zahlreiche Debatten über die Frage gibt, ob diese Statuen zu Lebzeiten des Buddha entstanden, steht außer Zweifel, dass es zu Buddhas Zeit in Indien viele große religiöse Traditionen gab wie den Brahmanismus und Jainismus sowie weitere bedeutende spirituelle Traditionen, die Kunstwerke hervorbrachten. Alle spirituellen Traditionen begehen ihre besonderen Festlichkeiten und Ereignisse mit großen Bauten oder mit anderen Kunstwerken. So hat auch der Buddhismus seine eigenen Anlässe für Gedenktage und Feste. Einige der frühen buddhistischen Kunstwerke sind die Monumente, die sich im Lauf der Jahre zur besonderen Kunstform, den *Stupas*, entwickelt haben. Es scheint, dass die Anhänger des Buddha kurze Zeit nach seinem Hinscheiden an dem in Nordindien gelegenen Ort Kushinagar, wo der Buddha eingeäschert wurde, ein Monument errichteten. Dabei handelt es sich vielleicht um den frühesten *Stupa*, einen massiven Hügel, dem nach und nach andere Bauten hinzugefügt wurden. Entsprechend der damaligen Tradition baute man damals *Stupas*, nachdem die Asche Buddhas unter seinen engsten Jüngern und den in der Gegend ansässigen Königen verteilt worden war. In den *Stupas* wurde die Asche Buddhas an einem sicheren Ort verwahrt, an dem die Öffentlichkeit ihm Respekt erweisen und ihn verehren konnte. Ursprünglich waren *Stupas* massive Grabhügel von unterschiedlicher Größe, aus Ziegeln erbaut oder aus einfachen riesigen Erdhügeln bestehend. In der Mitte befindet sich ein Schrein aus Metall, Stein oder Lehm, der für die Asche bestimmt ist und um den herum der Bau errichtet wurde. Später, als sich der Buddhismus nach Süden und Osten in Sri Lanka, Burma, Thailand und Indonesien wie auch nach Norden und Westen in Kaschmir, Afghanistan, Nepal, Tibet und weiter nach China und Japan ausbreitete, traten verschiedene Formen und Strukturen und eine große Vielfalt von Stilen der *Stupas* in Erscheinung. Heute sieht man viele verschiedene Arten von *Stupas* in diesen Ländern und die Tradition, sie zu religiösen Zwecken zu nutzen, ist nach wie vor in allen buddhistischen Ländern und an buddhistischen Orten lebendig. Eine andere buddhistische Kunstform besteht in Bildern und Skulpturen, die Buddha darstellen. Man sagt, dass in den Anfängen des Buddhismus, etwa in den ersten Jahrhunderten, keine Bilder Buddhas existierten. Der Verehrung und dem Andenken an den Buddha und seine Lehren dienten Bilder des Bodhi-Baums, das Rad, das den *Dharma* darstellt, der Fußabdruck Buddhas oder der Lotus von tiefer symbolischer Bedeutung. Erst später entstanden Bilder Buddhas.

Die geographische Ausbreitung des Buddhismus und die Entwicklung buddhistischen Denkens brachten verschiedene Traditionen hervor, die manchmal als südliche und nördliche Traditionen bezeichnet werden oder als Theravada, darunter ist die früheste und älteste buddhistische Tradition zu verstehen, und Mahayana-Tradition. Diese verschiedenen Traditionen des Buddhismus fanden verschiedene Interpretationen in der buddhistischen Bildwelt und innerhalb dieser Traditionen entwickelten sich viele Stile. Die frühesten bildlichen Darstellungen Buddhas sind Statuen aus Felsgestein, Holz oder Lehm. Später wurden die Statuen aus Metall gemacht, aus Bronze, Silber wie auch Gold. Die Statuen aus den verschiedenen Traditionen, die sich durch Größe und Stil unterscheiden, haben etwas gemeinsam: Die Abbildungen erheben nicht den Anspruch, genaue Darstellungen des Buddha zu sein; sie zeigen nicht, wie er tatsächlich zu Lebzeiten ausgesehen hat. Im Allgemeinen werden alle diese Abbildungen dazu benutzt, seine Lehren zu veranschaulichen und damit sind folglich seine Lehren von Mitgefühl und Weisheit gemeint. Wenn wir alle diese Statuen betrachten, die im Lauf von tausend Jahren und in weit voneinander entfernten Gebieten entstanden, so überrascht uns die große Ähnlichkeit der Haltungen und Gesten. Die verschiedenen Traditionen und Stile weisen in der Darstellung der Züge des Buddha einen gemeinsamen Ausdruck auf. Der freundliche Blick seiner weit geöffneten Augen soll Mitgefühl ausdrücken, seine rechte Hand berührt die Erde zum Zeichen der Überwindung von Elementen wie Verblendung, Begehren, Abneigung oder Unwissenheit. Oft wird er sitzend in meditierender Haltung dargestellt. Dieser Ausdruck und diese Haltung sind häufig zu finden. Alle diese Darstellungen dienen dazu, unser Verständnis seiner Lehren über Mitgefühl und Weisheit zu vertiefen und uns daran zu erinnern, dass wir diese Form des erwachten Geistes in uns selbst entwickeln. Darstellungen des Buddha zeigen ihn sitzend, stehend, gehend und mit verschiedenen Handbewegungen. Alle diese Ausdrucksformen des Körpers veranschaulichen, dass jedes Lebewesen die Fähigkeit besitzt, Mitgefühl und Weisheit zu entwickeln. Wie die moderne Psychologie eine Wissenschaft der Körpersprache entwickelt hat, der zu Folge die Haltung einer Person etwas über ihre inneren Vorgänge aussagt, so verhält es sich mit den verschiedenen Handbewegungen und Bewegungen wie Gehen, Sitzen und Liegen. Sie stellen spontane Regungen innerer Bewusstheit von Mitgefühl und Weisheit dar. Jede dieser Gesten hat eine eigene Bedeutung und alle diese Gesten sind keine erfundenen künstlichen, sondern spontane natürliche Ausdrucksformen, die über kulturelle Schranken hinweg eine starke Anziehungskraft auf uns ausüben. Damit verbunden ist die Hoffnung, dass die Betrachtung buddhistischer Kunstwerke beim Leser eine Saite zum Klingen bringt, einen Klang hervorruft, der in uns die Bereitschaft zum spontanen Ausdruck von Mitgefühl und Weisheit weckt.

Geshe Tashi Tsering,
buddhistischer Mönch aus Tibet,
Lehrer am Jamyang Buddhist Centre

La sagesse et la compassion exprimées par les arts

Voici environ 2 500 ans, un jeune garçon naquit dans la famille royale d'un pays à cheval sur ce qui est aujourd'hui le nord de l'Inde et le sud du Népal. Il fut prénommé Siddharta. Destiné à une vie de luxe princier, il possédait une quantité de biens temporels pour sa jouissance, des objets d'art, d'immenses richesses, des éléphants, des chevaux, des serviteurs et ainsi de suite. Il s'adonnait en outre à toutes sortes d'activités royales agréables. Il se maria et eut un fils mais, vers l'âge de 27 ans, Siddharta commença à chercher la vérité sur la nature de la vie. C'est alors que, suivant la coutume de l'époque, il renonça à la vie de ce monde et se consacra à la quête de cette vérité. Il quitta la sécurité de ses palais, son épouse et son fils, ainsi que toutes ses sources de plaisir et se mit en route pour trouver la vérité sur la nature de la vie. Pendant de longues années, il chercha une réponse à cette question, il rencontra un grand nombre de maîtres pleins de sagesse et étudia leurs réponses à son interrogation. Il pratiqua maintes méthodes de méditation et la plus grande austérité, jusqu'au jour où il se rendit compte que l'austérité et l'ascèse ne permettent pas à elles seules de découvrir le sens qu'il recherchait. Finalement, il partit et s'assit sous un pippal (figuier des pagodes) et fit le vœu de ne plus bouger tant qu'il n'aurait pas reçu de réponse. C'est là que sa quête parvint à son stade final et qu'il trouva la réponse tant attendue. Ce n'était pas un simple raisonnement intellectuel mais un processus qui le conduisit à s'éveiller complètement à la nature de la réalité, notamment à celle de cette vie. Cette expérience extraordinaire lui valut le surnom de Bouddha. En sanscrit, « bouddha » veut dire « l'Éveillé ». Être éveillé signifie que l'esprit a reçu l'illumination, sous la forme d'une compassion et d'une sagesse infinies – une sagesse concernant la vraie nature de la réalité et une compassion qui englobe tous les êtres vivants. Ce sont ces qualités auxquelles il est fait référence ici dans le mot « bouddha » – être éveillé. Grâce à son esprit éveillé, le Bouddha enseigna pendant presque 45 à 46 ans, jusqu'à son dernier jour. Son enseignement visait avant tout à cultiver en chaque être vivant la compassion et la sagesse, selon ses capacités. Ce type de compassion et même de sagesse sont des pratiques très courantes dans toutes les religions du monde.

Ce qui fait le caractère exceptionnel du bouddhisme, c'est que ces pratiques n'impliquent pas de croire à un être supra-naturel, à un créateur, il s'agit simplement de reconnaître que chaque être vivant possède le potentiel pour devenir un être pleinement éveillé s'il cultive la compassion et la sagesse. Commencer par la non-violence, telle est l'essence de cette pratique de la compassion, l'une des leçons les plus essentielles que le Bouddha nous ait données. La non-violence ne se réduit pas à éviter la violence physique ou verbale, à éviter de détruire la paix et le bonheur des autres peuples et des autres hommes. Ici, la pratique de la non-violence se concentre avant tout sur la violence intérieure. Le but est de comprendre et de s'opposer à ce qui dans le bouddhisme est appelé les trois poisons : désir, haine et ignorance. Ce sont les trois sources de l'impulsion conduisant à la violence physique et verbale. Aussi, selon la croyance bouddhiste, la violence extérieure vient de celle qui est en nous et, tant que nous n'avons pas appris à maîtriser la violence intérieure, autrement dit le désir, la haine et l'ignorance, nous ne parviendrons pas aussi bien à éviter la violence extérieure et nous peinerons à instaurer une paix durable. C'est pourquoi, dans le bouddhisme, la pratique de la compassion équivaut en grande partie à maîtriser ces états spirituels malsains. La racine de ces états est considérée comme une ignorance fondamentale de la nature, la nôtre comme celle des autres phénomènes. C'est de cette ignorance que résultent le désir, la haine et toutes les émotions négatives qui s'ensuivent. Le secret pour maîtriser cette ignorance fondamentale, c'est développer sa sagesse, de l'équanimité de base jusqu'à la pleine connaissance des modes les plus subtils de notre existence. Ces états intellectuels malsains ou faussés, tels que le désir, la haine et l'ignorance, et les émotions négatives qu'ils entraînent, surviennent naturellement en l'absence de sagesse. La sagesse ici signifie voir les choses et les événements tels qu'ils sont vraiment, sans exagération et sans vaines attentes. Cultiver cette façon de voir les choses et les événements tels qu'ils sont réellement est la connaissance la plus importante que nous puissions acquérir dans le contexte de la sagesse et c'est la qualité la plus essentielle pour contrer la violence intérieure. Par conséquent, l'association de la compassion et de la sagesse est primordiale. C'est le développement de la compassion en vue de s'attaquer dès la racine à la violence intérieure, puis de la traiter et de l'éliminer par la culture de la sagesse. Cela est appelé l'union de la sagesse et de la compassion et c'est le message essentiel transmis par le Bouddha à ses disciples.

Les nombreux arts bouddhiques expriment très clairement ces deux qualités, la sagesse et la compassion, par leurs manifestations dans des disciplines telles que la sculpture et la construction de *stupas*. Les œuvres d'art bouddhique ne sont pas des objets de culte, mais sont produites surtout pour accroître en chaque être humain la conscience de son potentiel intérieur pour devenir un être pleinement éveillé, pour se libérer de l'ignorance et parvenir à l'illumination. Elles expriment le parcours depuis l'ignorance

jusqu'à l'illumination. Même si un vif débat oppose les historiens sur la question de l'existence ou non de statues du Bouddha de son vivant, il est hors de doute qu'à cette époque un grand nombre de traditions religieuses cohabitaient en Inde, comme le brahmanisme et le jaïnisme, ainsi que d'autres traditions spirituelles majeures dont les arts étaient très évolués. Toutes les traditions spirituelles célèbrent leurs fêtes particulières grâce à des édifices ou à des arts magnifiques. De même, le bouddhisme commémore ou fête ses propres événements particuliers. Certaines des œuvres d'art bouddhique parmi les plus anciennes sont les monuments qui au fil du temps ont pris la forme du *stupa*. Peu de temps après le décès du Bouddha, ses disciples – dit-on – élevèrent un monument à l'endroit où il fut incinéré, à Kusinagara, dans le nord de l'Inde. Ce fut sans doute le premier *stupa* bouddhique, une colline qui fut peu à peu entourée par d'autres édifices. Conformément à la tradition de l'époque, quand les cendres du Bouddha furent dispersées entre ses disciples les plus proches et les rois de cette région, c'est tout naturellement que ceux-ci firent édifier des *stupas*. Ils offraient un lieu pour conserver ces reliques que le public pouvait venir contempler afin de vénérer le Bouddha. À l'origine, les *stupas* n'étaient que d'énormes monticules pleins et de taille variable, construits en briques ou simplement en terre. L'édifice était élevé autour d'une boîte en métal, en pierre ou en argile, placée au centre et qui renfermait les cendres. Par la suite, les styles évoluèrent et les formes se diversifièrent avec la progression du bouddhisme vers le sud et l'est au Sri Lanka, en Birmanie, en Thaïlande et en Indonésie, mais aussi au nord et à l'ouest, au Cachemire, en Afghanistan, au Népal, au Tibet et jusqu'en Chine et au Japon. De nos jours, nous pouvons y contempler différents types de *stupas* qui sont toujours très utilisés dans un but religieux dans tous les pays et régions bouddhistes. Le dessin et la sculpture d'images du Bouddha sont deux autres formes d'art bouddhique. Dans les premiers temps du bouddhisme, à ce qu'il paraît, le Bouddha n'était pas représenté. Afin de le commémorer et de se rappeler sa personne et ses leçons, les fidèles se servaient entre autres d'images du figuier pippal, de la roue représentant le *dharma* du Bouddha, de l'empreinte du pied du Bouddha ou du lotus à forte connotation symbolique. L'iconographie du Bouddha est apparue à une date ultérieure.

L'expansion géographique du bouddhisme et l'évolution de sa pensée ont abouti à deux grandes voies, parfois appelées traditions du Sud et du Nord ou encore Theravada, pour la plus ancienne, et Mahayana. Elles ont naturellement livré des interprétations divergentes de l'iconographie bouddhique, ainsi que des styles qui leur sont propres. Dans la statuaire antique, les images du Bouddha étaient sculptées dans la pierre et le bois ou façonnées en argile. Plus tard, les sculpteurs utilisèrent des métaux, le bronze et l'argent aussi bien que l'or. Cependant, quels que soient le style et la taille, les traditions ont un point commun : ces productions ne sont pas supposées être des représentations précises du Bouddha, ni ne sont supposées le montrer tel qu'il fut au cours de sa vie. Elles visent en général à exprimer ses leçons, et donc, bien entendu, ce qu'il nous a appris sur la compassion et la sagesse. Un fait surprenant, quand on contemple toutes ces statues exécutées au fil des millénaires et séparées par des distances considérables, est la similitude frappante entre les principales postures et les gestes. Par ailleurs, les différentes traditions et les styles représentent tous la même expression sur le visage du Bouddha. Ses yeux ouverts au regard très doux expriment sa compassion, sa main droite touche la terre pour démontrer qu'il a surmonté les déceptions, le désir, la haine, l'ignorance, et ainsi de suite. Il est souvent assis en position de méditation. Ce type d'expression et de posture se retrouve partout. Toutes ces représentations sont ici pour prouver et approfondir notre connaissance de ses enseignements sur la compassion et la sagesse, et pour nous rappeler que nous aussi pouvons cultiver en nous-mêmes ce type d'éveil spirituel. L'art bouddhique nous montre le Bouddha assis, debout, en train de marcher, ses mains adoptant différentes positions. Toutes ces expressions corporelles, en fait très spontanées, cherchent à expliquer que chaque être vivant possède le potentiel requis pour éprouver la compassion et la sagesse. Tout comme la psychologie moderne a mis au point une science du langage corporel pour interpréter l'état mental d'une personne à travers ses postures, les gestes des mains et les activités du Bouddha, selon qu'il marche, est assis ou couché, révèlent ce qu'il ressent. Ce sont toutes des expressions naturelles et spontanées de la pureté de l'éveil intérieur à la sagesse et à la compassion. Toutes ont une signification différente et ces gestes ne se limitent pas à des expressions artificielles, mais conservent une spontanéité et un naturel qui nous touchent profondément, même au-delà des frontières culturelles. Espérons que la présente étude de ces œuvres d'art bouddhique saura profondément toucher le lecteur et le sensibiliser aux expressions spontanées et naturelles de la compassion et de la sagesse en chacun de nous.

Geshe Tashi Tsering,
moine bouddhiste tibétain,
professeur en résidence au centre bouddhiste Jamyang

La sabiduría y la compasión expresadas a través de las artes

Hace unos 2.500 años, un muchacho llamado Siddhartha nació en el seno de la familia real de un principado que se extendía por lo que actualmente es el norte de la India y el sur de Nepal. Fue criado en una vida de lujos y disponía de todo tipo de comodidades mundanas: un palacio, sirvientes, elefantes y caballos, bellos objetos y riquezas diversas. Asimismo disfrutaba de infinidad de placenteras actividades cortesanas. Estaba casado y tenia un hijo. Pero a la edad de 27 años, Siddhartha empezó a preguntarse por la verdad sobre la naturaleza de la existencia. Y fue entonces, cuando siguiendo la costumbre de aquellos tiempos, renunció a la vida de la corte y se dedicó a la búsqueda de la verdad. Abandonó a su mujer y a su hijo, la seguridad de palacio, así como todas sus posesiones y actividades placenteras, y se puso en camino en pos de la verdad de la naturaleza de la vida. Durante mucho tiempo buscó la respuesta a esta cuestión como discípulo de sabios maestros de su tiempo. Asimismo practicó la meditación y vivió con gran austeridad, hasta que finalmente cayó en la cuenta de que la sobriedad y el ascetismo por sí mismos no le iban a ayudar a hallar lo que estaba buscando. Entonces, como ya es conocido, acudió a sentarse bajo el árbol de Bodhi y prometió no moverse de allí hasta haber resuelto la cuestión. De esa forma consiguió por fin su objetivo y dio con la solución a sus inquietudes. La respuesta no era una mera cuestión intelectual, sino un proceso que le llevaría a un despertar a la naturaleza de la realidad, incluyendo la naturaleza de su existencia. Y por esa gran revelación recibió el nombre de Buda. Y es que "Buddha" en sánscrito significa literalmente "el despierto". En este contexto, "estar despierto" implica que su mente alcanzó la plena consciencia a través de la compasión y la sabiduría; la compasión para con todos los seres vivos y la sabiduría sobre la verdadera naturaleza de la realidad. Ésas son las virtudes a las que se refiere la palabra "Buddha". Así, con su actitud despierta y consciente, el Buda impartió sus enseñanzas durante 45 ó 46 años hasta su muerte, orientando sus doctrinas principalmente a cultivar en cada ser vivo la compasión y la sabiduría de acuerdo con su capacidad. Este tipo de compasión e incluso de sabiduría son comunes a todas las religiones del mundo.

La peculiaridad del budismo reside en que esas prácticas se acometen sin creer en un ser eterno sobrenatural ni afirmar la existencia de un creador, sino simplemente mediante el convencimiento de que todos y cada uno de los seres vivos poseen en sí mismos el potencial de convertirse en criaturas plenamente conscientes por medio de la práctica de la compasión y la sabiduría. La esencia de la compasión reside en primer lugar en la no violencia, una de las bases de las doctrinas que nos legó el Buda. En este contexto, la no violencia no sólo implica evitar las agresiones físicas o verbales, la destrucción de la paz y la felicidad de otras personas y seres; también significa enfrentarse a la propia violencia interior. El objetivo es lograr la comprensión y contrarrestar lo que en el budismo se denominan los tres venenos: apego, aversión e ignorancia. De ellos proviene la fuerza de la que se deriva el impulso para la violencia exterior física o verbal. Por tanto, en el budismo existe la creencia de que la violencia externa procede de la violencia interna y de que si no se aprende a controlar las fuerzas negativas interiores, como el apego, la aversión y la ignorancia, la mera supresión de los factores exteriores no es fructífera y no conlleva la paz definitiva. Por eso en el budismo, la práctica de la compasión es mucho más que el intento de mantener bajo control los estados insanos mentales internos. Se considera que el origen de esos estados es una comprensión errónea de nuestra propia naturaleza y nuestros fenómenos, y que la ignorancia es la madre del apego y la aversión, y de todas las emociones negativas consecuencia de ellas. La clave para acabar con esa ignorancia esencial es el desarrollo de la sabiduría, partiendo de una ecuanimidad básica hasta llegar al conocimiento total de los más sutiles modos de nuestra existencia. Esos estados insanos o distorsionados como el apego, la aversión y la ignorancia, y las emociones negativas inherentes a ellos surgen por tanto de una forma natural en ausencia de sabiduría. La sabiduría implica en este caso la capacidad de ver las cosas y los eventos como realmente son, sin exageraciones ni expectativas innecesarias. El cultivo de esta forma de considerar la realidad y los acontecimientos en su justa dimensión es el objetivo principal a alcanzar en el contexto de la sabiduría y la cualidad más importante a cultivar para contrarrestar la violencia interna. Por eso, la clave está en la combinación de la compasión y la sabiduría; en el desarrollo de la compasión al reducir la violencia interna al principio, combatirla después y finalmente eliminarla por completo gracias al fomento de la sabiduría. Esto es lo que se denomina la unión entre sabiduría y compasión, que constituye el núcleo del mensaje y las enseñanzas que el Buda impartió a sus seguidores.

El arte budista en sus diversas manifestaciones expresa muy claramente esas dos virtudes, la sabiduría y la compasión, a través de esculturas y *estupas*. Sus obras de arte no son objetos de devoción, sino que tienen como meta principal aumentar en lo más profundo de todos y cada uno de los humanos la consciencia sobre el propio potencial para convertirse en seres realmente despiertos y libres de ignorancia, y alcanzar así la iluminación. Los objetos de arte budista expresan por tanto la trayectoria desde la

ignorancia hasta la iluminación. Aunque hay un gran debate entre los historiadores sobre si en vida del Buda había estatuas de su persona, no hay duda de que ya por aquel entonces la India tenía una antigua tradición religiosa con el brahmanismo, el jainismo y otras doctrinas espirituales de importancia con artes bien desarrolladas. Todos los movimientos espirituales celebran festividades y acontecimientos especiales por medio de grandes construcciones y del arte en general. Al igual que ellos, el budismo tiene sus propios eventos que conmemorar o festejar. Algunas de sus primeras obras de arte fueron monumentos que con los años evolucionaron hasta adoptar la forma artística de la *estupa*. Parece ser que poco después del fallecimiento del Buda, sus seguidores construyeron un monumento en Kushinagar, un lugar al norte de la India en el que el maestro había sido incinerado. Ésa fue quizás la primera *estupa* budista, un sólido montículo que gradualmente se fue rodeando de otras construcciones. Como era la costumbre por aquel entonces, las cenizas del Buda se repartieron entre sus más allegados discípulos y reyes de la región, quienes construyeron una especie de mausoleos para custodiarlas. Las *estupas* eran lugares seguros en los que conservar los restos del Buda para que el público pudiera presentarle sus respetos y venerarlo. Originalmente estas construcciones eran simples y sólidos montículos de diferente –pero siempre considerable– tamaño construidos con ladrillos o simplemente formados por un montón de tierra, en cuyo centro se guardaba un cofre de metal, piedra o arcilla que contenía las cenizas. Con el tiempo, las diferentes formas y construcciones fueron evolucionando y surgieron *estupas* en una infinidad de estilos a medida que el budismo se fue extendiendo hacia el sur y el este por Sri Lanka, Burma, Tailandia e Indonesia, y también hacia el norte y el oeste por tierras de Cachemira, Afganistán, Nepal, el Tíbet e incluso de China y Japón. Hoy en día se pueden encontrar muchos modelos diferentes de *estupas* en esos países y la vibrante tradición de usarlos con fines religiosos aún florece en todos ellos. Otro tipo de arte budista es el de los dibujos y esculturas de la imagen del maestro. Al parecer en los primeros tiempos del budismo, quizás los primeros cien años, no existían imágenes de su persona. Para conmemorar y recordar al Buda y sus enseñanzas, las representaciones que se usaban eran, entre otras, el árbol de Bodhi, la rueda del *dharma*, la huella del pie del maestro o la flor de loto de profundo simbolismo. Sólo posteriormente surgieron representaciones del propio Buda.

La expansión geográfica y el desarrollo del budismo tuvieron como consecuencia el nacimiento de diferentes corrientes. En ocasiones se diferencia entre tradiciones del norte y del sur, Theravada –la más antigua práctica budista–, y el budismo Mahayana. Naturalmente los distintos movimientos han producido sendas interpretaciones de la imaginería y muchos estilos diferenciados. En las primeras representaciones de la imagen del Buda, las estatuas eran de piedra, madera o arcilla. Posteriormente se empezaron a realizar en metal: bronce, plata e incluso oro. Pero todas estas estatuas de diversos tamaños y estilos poseen una cosa en común: las imágenes producidas no son representaciones exactas del Buda y no muestran qué aspecto tenía en vida, sino que por lo general, se usan más bien para simbolizar su doctrina, es decir, sus enseñanzas sobre la compasión y la sabiduría. Cuando observamos todas estas esculturas creadas a lo largo de milenios y separadas por vastas distancias geográficas constatamos un hecho sorprendente: la enorme similitud de posturas y gestos básicos. Las tradiciones y estilos diferentes también comparten una misma expresión en la representación del rostro del Buda: sus ojos abiertos tienen una mirada fija y amable que expresa compasión. Por otro lado, la mano derecha está en contacto con la tierra para demostrar que el maestro se encuentra más allá de engaños, apegos, aversiones e ignorancia. Además suele aparecer sentado en la postura de la meditación. La expresión y la postura son comunes a todas las representaciones que sirven para manifestar y ahondar nuestro entendimiento de sus enseñanzas sobre la compasión y la sabiduría, y para recordarnos que todos podemos alcanzar también esa mente consciente por nosotros mismos. Las representaciones del Buda lo muestran sentado, de pie, caminando, y con diferentes gestos de las manos. Esas posturas corporales son expresiones de gran espontaneidad como reflejo de que todos y cada uno de los seres vivos disponen del potencial de sentir compasión y sabiduría. Al igual que la moderna psicología ha desarrollado una ciencia del lenguaje corporal que a través de las posturas de una persona entrevé lo que sucede en su mente, la posición de las manos, y la actitud de caminar, estar sentado o yacer son expresiones espontáneas y naturales de una prístina conciencia interna de sabiduría y compasión. Cada uno de esos gestos tiene un significado diferente y no es reflejo de una manifestación artificial, sino de una expresión natural con una profunda capacidad de apelación incluso más allá de las fronteras culturales. Esperemos que el estudio de las artes budistas tenga en el lector una profunda resonancia que vibre en consonancia con la expresión natural de la compasión y la sabiduría en todos nosotros.

Geshe Tashi Tsering,
monje budista tibetano,
profesor residente del Centro Budista Jamyang

Saggezza e compassione espresse attraverso l'arte

Circa 2500 anni or sono, un giovane di nome Siddhartha nacque in una famiglia di stirpe reale che regnava su parte dell'attuale India settentrionale e del Nepal meridionale. Il giovane viveva circondato da ogni lusso che la sua condizione reale gli potesse offrire. Possedeva beni mondani quali palazzi, magnifici oggetti, grandi ricchezze, elefanti, cavalli, servitori e prendeva parte a ogni genere di piacevole attività regale. Benché sposato e padre di un figlio, intorno ai 27 anni Siddhartha si mise alla ricerca della verità sulla natura della vita. Fu allora che, secondo gli usi dell'epoca, rinunciò alla vita mondana e si votò alla ricerca della verità, lasciandosi alle spalle le certezze del proprio palazzo, la moglie e il figlio, nonché tutti i piaceri dati dagli oggetti e dalle attività terrene per andare alla ricerca della vera natura della vita. Per lungo tempo cercò una risposta a questo quesito, seguendo molti maestri spirituali della sua epoca e studiando le loro risposte alle domande su quale fosse la natura di questa vita. Praticò a fondo la meditazione e visse con estrema austerità finché non comprese che l'austerità e l'ascetismo in sé non erano il mezzo per scoprire il significato di quanto cercava. Alla fine, come è noto, si sedette sotto l'albero della Bodhi e giurò che non si sarebbe mosso finché la sua ricerca non si fosse conclusa. Fu allora che la sua ricerca diede i frutti definitivi; la risposta che trovò non era una mera forma di comprensione intellettuale, bensì un processo che lo portò ad acquistare una profonda consapevolezza della natura della realtà e della vita. Fu proprio a causa di questa consapevolezza che venne chiamato il Buddha. "Buddha" in sanscrito significa "il risvegliato", a indicare che la sua mente era divenuta pienamente capace di grande compassione e di saggezza; una saggezza che svela la vera natura della realtà e una compassione rivolta a tutte le creature viventi. Sono queste le qualità a cui ci si riferisce qui con il nome Buddha, il Risvegliato. Grazie a tale esperienza di risveglio, il Buddha insegnò per circa 45–46 anni fino alla sua morte. I suoi insegnamenti erano principalmente diretti a coltivare la compassione e la saggezza in ogni creatura vivente secondo le possibilità di ognuno. La compassione e la saggezza sono insegnamenti diffusi in tutte le religioni del mondo.

Ciò che rende unico il Buddhismo è che tali pratiche vengono svolte senza credere in un essere soprannaturale eterno, senza dunque sostenere l'esistenza di un creatore ma semplicemente riconoscendo che ogni essere vivente possiede il potenziale di divenire un essere "risvegliato" qualora gli riesca di coltivare la compassione e la saggezza. Il punto di partenza di questa pratica della compassione è la nonviolenza, uno degli insegnamenti essenziali che il Buddha ci ha trasmesso. Nonviolenza non significa solamente rifuggire la violenza fisica e verbale o rispettare la pace e la felicità di altre persone o esseri viventi, bensì affrontare la violenza interiore. Il compito essenziale è di comprendere e opporsi a ciò che nel Buddhismo sono considerati i tre veleni: la cupidigia, la collera e l'ignoranza. Essi rappresentano la fonte da cui deriva l'impulso della violenza esteriore fisica e verbale; secondo il credo buddhista, dunque, la violenza esteriore deriva dalla violenza interiore e fintanto che non si impari ad affrontare la violenza interiore, provocata da cupidigia, collera e ignoranza, il semplice fatto di evitare la violenza esteriore non potrà dare frutti, né essere fonte di pace duratura. Pertanto nel Buddhismo la pratica della compassione consiste essenzialmente nell'occuparsi di tali stati mentali interiori. Le radici di questi stati sono viste come un sostanziale fraintendimento della natura di noi stessi e di altri fenomeni. È dall'ignoranza che provengono la cupidigia, la collera e tutte le emozioni negative che ne derivano. La chiave per affrontare questa fondamentale ignoranza è di sviluppare la saggezza, dalla serenità d'animo fino alla comprensione delle sfumature più sottili della nostra esistenza. Questi stati mentali malsani e distorti, quali sono la cupidigia, la collera e l'ignoranza, nonché le emozioni negative che comportano, si affermano spontaneamente in assenza di saggezza, intesa come capacità di vedere le cose e gli eventi così come sono realmente, senza esagerazioni e inutili aspettative. La forma di comprensione più importante da sviluppare nel contesto della saggezza è la capacità di abbracciare questo modo di vedere le cose e gli eventi così come essi sono in realtà; questa è anche la qualità da coltivare per contrastare la violenza interiore. È dunque imprescindibile la combinazione di saggezza e compassione al fine di ridurre inizialmente la violenza interiore, per poi contrastarla e infine eliminarla grazie allo sviluppo della saggezza. Questa è definita l'unione di saggezza e compassione ed è il messaggio e l'insegnamento centrale che il Buddha lasciò ai propri seguaci.

Le molteplici manifestazioni dell'arte buddhista esprimono in maniera estremamente chiara queste due qualità, la saggezza e la compassione, attraverso opere d'arte scultoree e lo sviluppo degli *stupa*. I beni artistici buddhisti non sono oggetti di culto; vengono realizzati principalmente per incrementare in ogni essere umano la consapevolezza del potenziale interiore che porta al completo risveglio, allo scopo di liberarsi dall'ignoranza e di raggiungere l'illuminazione. Tali oggetti artistici sono l'espressione del viaggio dall'ignoranza all'illuminazione. A dispetto di un acceso dibattito tra gli storici sul fatto che esistessero o meno statue del Buddha quando questi era ancora in vita, non vi è alcun dubbio che all'epoca del Buddha in India vi fossero molte grandi reli-

gioni, quali il brahmanesimo e il giainismo, e altre importanti tradizioni spirituali con espressioni artistiche ben sviluppate. Tutte le tradizioni spirituali celebrano le proprie festività e gli eventi speciali attraverso grandi edifici o altre espressioni artistiche; proprio come tutte le tradizioni spirituali, anche il Buddhismo ha i propri eventi simbolici da commemorare e celebrare. Tra le prime espressioni artistiche buddhiste vi sono i monumenti che nel corso degli anni si sono sviluppati nella forma d'arte dello *stupa*. Secondo la tradizione, poco dopo la morte del Buddha, i suoi seguaci costruirono un monumento nel luogo in cui era stato cremato nel distretto di Kushinagar in India settentrionale. Questo fu probabilmente il primo *stupa* buddhista: una collinetta che venne progressivamente circondata da altre strutture. Come previsto dagli usi dell'epoca, le ceneri del Buddha vennero divise tra alcuni dei suoi discepoli più stretti e i re della zona; era pertanto naturale che a loro volta essi costruissero degli *stupa*, che conservavano le ceneri del Buddha in un luogo sicuro dove il pubblico poteva giungere a ossequiarlo e venerarlo. Originariamente questi non erano che massicce montagnole di varie dimensioni, realizzate in mattoni o semplicemente con grandi quantitativi di terra. Al centro vi era una scatola in metallo, pietra o argilla in cui erano riposte le ceneri e attorno a cui si sviluppava la struttura. Successivamente si vennero a creare altre forme e strutture e nacque una grande varietà di stili, a mano a mano che il Buddhismo si diffondeva nel Sud e nell'Est dello Sri Lanka, della Birmania, della Thailandia e dell'Indonesia, nonché nel Nord e nell'Ovest del Kashmir, dell'Afghanistan, del Nepal, del Tibet fino alla Cina e al Giappone. Oggigiorno è possibile osservare una grande varietà di *stupa* in tutti questi paesi; l'affermata tradizione di usarli per scopi religiosi è ancora fiorente in tutti i paesi e le località buddhiste. Un'altra espressione artistica tipica sono i disegni e le sculture del Buddha. Si narra che agli albori del Buddhismo, forse per diversi secoli, non esistessero rappresentazioni iconografiche del Buddha; per commemorare e ricordare il Buddha e i suoi insegnamenti venivano usate le immagini dell'albero della Bodhi, la ruota che rappresenta il *Dharma* del Buddha, l'impronta del Buddha o il loto, ricco di significati simbolici, nonché altri simboli. Solo successivamente vennero realizzate immagini del Buddha.

La diffusione geografica del Buddhismo e lo sviluppo del pensiero buddhista ha prodotto tradizioni differenti chiamate Buddhismo settentrionale e Buddhismo meridionale oppure anche Theravada − la prima tradizione o il Buddhismo degli Anziani − e Mahayana. Queste differenti tradizioni buddhiste hanno naturalmente dato origine a differenti interpretazioni dell'immaginario buddhista e molti stili si sono sviluppati all'interno di questa tradizione. Le prime rappresentazioni del Buddha erano costituite da statue in pietra, legno o argilla; successivamente queste vennero realizzate in metallo, bronzo, argento e anche oro. Le varie tradizioni con le diverse dimensioni e gli stili differenti hanno una cosa in comune: le immagini realizzate non intendono essere rappresentazioni fedeli del Buddha; non vogliono cioè mostrare quello che era l'aspetto del Buddha in vita, ma servono per esprimere i suoi insegnamenti, ossia la compassione e la saggezza. Un fatto sorprendente quando guardiamo tutte queste statue realizzate nel corso dei millenni e in aree geografiche lontanissime tra loro è la somiglianza tra le posture e i gesti assunti più frequentemente. Nella rappresentazione del volto del Buddha, le diverse tradizioni e i vari stili si ritrovano tutte nella medesima espressione. Gli occhi sono aperti in uno sguardo gentile che ne esprime la compassione, la sua mano destra tocca la terra per dimostrare che ha superato le illusioni, la cupidigia, la collera, l'ignoranza e via dicendo; inoltre viene spesso rappresentato seduto, in posizione di meditazione. Questo genere di espressione e di postura è comune a tutte le rappresentazioni che hanno la funzione di mostrarci e di rendere più profonda la comprensione dei suoi insegnamenti in merito alla compassione e alla saggezza e di ricordarci che anche noi possiamo coltivare dentro di noi un simile risveglio della mente. Le rappresentazioni del Buddha lo mostrano seduto, in piedi, in cammino e con diversi gesti della mano; tutte queste espressioni corporali sono espressioni spontanee che indicano come ogni creatura vivente possieda il potenziale per raggiungere la compassione e la saggezza. Proprio come la moderna psicologia ha sviluppato una scienza riguardo al linguaggio del corpo che spiega gli stati mentali interni di una persona attraverso la sua postura, lo stesso vale per tutti questi gesti della mano e per le posizioni in cammino, seduto e disteso. Sono tutte espressioni naturali e spontanee di una consapevolezza interna e immacolata della saggezza e della compassione. Ognuno di questi gesti ha diversi significati ed essi non sono atteggiamenti artificiosi, bensì espressioni naturali che costituiscono un forte richiamo in grado di superare qualsiasi barriera culturale. Mi auguro che lo studio di queste rappresentazioni artistiche buddhiste faccia vibrare corde profonde in ogni lettore, in armonia con le naturali espressioni della compassione e della saggezza dentro ognuno di noi.

Geshe Tashi Tsering,
monaco buddhista tibetano,
docente nel Jamyang Buddhist Centre

Our lives are in constant flux, which generates many predicaments. But when these are faced with a calm and clear mind supported by spiritual practice, they can all be successfully resolved.

Peace in the world depends on peace of mind, and peace of mind depends on an awareness that all human beings are members of a single family.

31

Transform your thoughts into positive ones. It is a mistake to think that everyone is bad. Some people are wicked, that is true, but that does not mean that everyone is.

The essence of all spiritual life is your emotion, your attitude towards others. Once you have pure and sincere motivation, all the rest follows.

No one can deny the material benefits of modern life, but we are still faced with suffering, fear and tension—perhaps more now than before.

Act cautiously. Above all, avoid becoming a Buddhist without reflecting on it first, without knowing anything about the religion but simply acting on a whim, only to find later on that this or that practice does not suit you or seems impossible.

It is as hard to see one's self as to look backwards without turning around.

In Tibetan, the word for blessing means transformation through majesty or power. In short, the meaning of blessing is to bring about, as a result of the experience, a transformation in one's mind for the better.

Romantic love is usually based on the illusion of a self and a demand for something back. Spiritual love, then, is altruistic love or universal love.

Right from the moment of our birth, we are under the care and kindness of our parents and then later on in our life, when we are oppressed by sickness and become old, we are again dependant on the kindness of others.

Real joy comes from giving and not caring about whether anyone ever knows or acknowledges it.

Be master of mind rather than be mastered by mind.

We must not lose sight of our fundamental goal.

I have found that the greatest degree of inner tranquillity comes from the development of love and compassion.

Love and compassion are what we must strive to cultivate in ourselves, extending their present boundaries all the way to limitlessness.

We think in generalities but we live in detail.

The goal of the practice is not to obtain miraculous powers but to transform our being.

Our own life is the instrument with which we experiment with truth.

අතිගරු ඩී. බී. විජේතුංග රනාධිපතිතුමා
රිසිස් සුරා කරණ ලදී

The days and nights are relentlessly passing. How well am I spending my time?

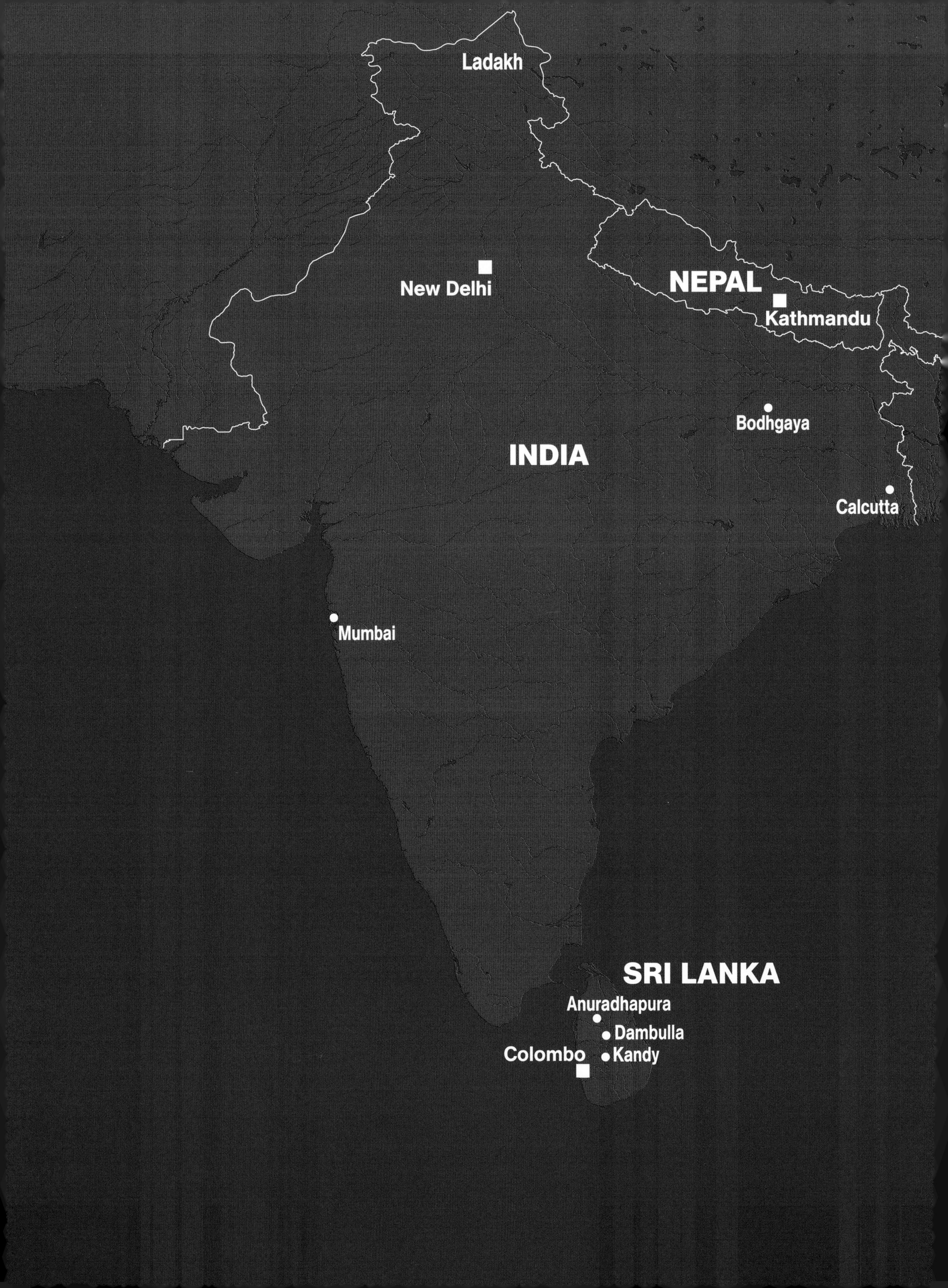
Ladakh
New Delhi
NEPAL
Kathmandu
Bodhgaya
INDIA
Calcutta
Mumbai
SRI LANKA
Anuradhapura
Dambulla
Colombo
Kandy

Dedicated to His Holiness the Dalai Lama and his office staff, Alexandra Bonnet who traveled with me on this trip and who has helped, supported and encouraged me throughout the project, my two lovely daughters, Katie and Georgia, to Richard Laing for his valuable help and advice, and all my friends (including the ones who thought that I was absolutely mad).

Robin Kyte-Coles

Robin Kyte-Coles was born in Kampala, Uganda. He has lived in the U.K., Mallorca, the Canary Islands and India doing a variety of different things apart from photography, including running an Ashtanga Yoga Shala. He felt inspired to work on a book about Buddhist culture while traveling to Asia for his handcrafted furniture business. He wrote to His Holiness the Dalai Lama, explaining his plans and asking him for his blessing and a letter of introduction, which he kindly granted. In spring 2007, Robin left the U.K. for three months of intense photography in South and Southeast Asia. This journey proved much more challenging than he had anticipated on many levels due to the heat and humidity that was hard on both the photographer and the equipment, the endless traveling, and the difficult lighting inside the temples. Robin's motivation for this project came from a genuine interest in Buddhist philosophy: "I have thought about what attracted me first to Buddhism and I think it is this: to be compassionate. To truly understand what compassion means and integrate it into one's daily life."

Robin Kyte-Coles wurde in Kampala, Uganda geboren. Er hat bereits an unterschiedlichen Orten gelebt, in Großbritannien, Mallorca, auf den Kanarischen Inseln sowie in Indien, und neben der Photographie verschiedene weitere Tätigkeiten ausgeübt, darunter die Leitung einer Ashtanga Yoga Shala. Die Anregung zu einem Buch über Buddhistische Kultur erhielt er in der Zeit, als er mit handgefertigten Möbeln handelte und geschäftlich in Asien unterwegs war. Er schrieb an Seine Heiligkeit den Dalai Lama, erläuterte ihm seine Pläne und bat ihn um seinen Segen und ein Empfehlungsschreiben, was dieser freundlich zusagte. Im Frühjahr 2007 verließ Robin Großbritannien, um drei Monate in Süd- und Südostasien zu photographieren. Diese Reise stellte unerwartet hohe Anforderungen an ihn, das betraf die Hitze und Feuchtigkeit, eine schwere Belastung für den Photographen und die Ausrüstung, das endlose Reisen und die schwierige Beleuchtung im Innern der Tempel. Robins Motivation entsprang einem ursprünglichen Interesse an buddhistischer Philosophie: „Wenn ich darüber nachdenke, was mich zuerst am Buddhismus angezogen hat, so ist es dies: Mitgefühl zu zeigen; wirklich zu verstehen, was Mitgefühl bedeutet und es zum Bestandteil des eigenen Alltags zu machen."

Robin Kyte-Coles est né à Kampala, en Ouganda. Il a vécu au Royaume-Uni, à Majorque, aux îles Canaries et en Inde et, outre la photographie, a exercé divers métiers et notamment dirigé une shala d'ashtanga yoga. C'est au cours de ses voyages en Asie pour son entreprise de mobilier artisanal que l'inspiration lui est venue d'un livre sur la culture bouddhique. Il a écrit à Sa Sainteté le Dalaï-Lama, lui expliquant ses projets et le priant de lui accorder sa bénédiction, ainsi qu'une lettre d'introduction, ce qui lui a été concédé très aimablement. Au printemps 2007, Robin a quitté le Royaume-Uni pour plusieurs mois de photographie intense en Asie du Sud et du Sud-Est. Le voyage s'est révélé beaucoup plus éprouvant qu'il ne l'aurait pensé, pour lui autant que pour son équipement, en raison notamment de la chaleur et de l'humidité, des périples sans fin, et des éclairages difficiles dans les temples. La motivation de Robin pour ce projet résulte d'un intérêt profond pour la philosophie bouddhiste : « J'ai réfléchi à ce qui m'a attiré en premier lieu dans le bouddhisme et je pense que c'est ceci : éprouver de la compassion. Comprendre vraiment ce que signifie la compassion et l'intégrer dans sa vie de tous les jours. »

Robin Kyte-Coles, nacido en Kampala (Uganda), ha vivido en Gran Bretaña, Mallorca, las Islas Canarias y la India, lugares en los que, a ademas de a la fotografía, se ha dedicado a muchas otras actividades, entre otras, la dirección de un centro Ashtanga Yoga Shala. La inspiración para realizar un libro sobre la cultura budista le llegó durante un viaje que hizo por Asia por razón de su negocio de muebles artesanos. Se dirigió por escrito a Su Santidad el Dalai Lama para explicarle el proyecto y solicitar su bendición y una carta de recomendación, y éste amablemente accedió. Así en la primavera del año 2007, Robin se ausentó tres meses de Gran Bretaña para realizar un intenso reportaje fotográfico por el sur y el sureste de Asia. El viaje fue un reto mayor del esperado en muchos sentidos debido al calor y a la humedad –que resultaron una dura prueba tanto para el fotógrafo como para el equipo–, a los continuos traslados y a la dificultad de iluminar el interior de los templos. La motivación de Robin para este proyecto emana de un genuino interés por la filosofía budista: "He reflexionado acerca de lo que en primera línea me atrajo del budismo y creo que fue lo siguiente: la virtud de ser compasivo, el verdadero entendimiento de lo que significa la compasión y su aplicación a la vida diaria."

Robin Kyte-Coles nasce a Kampala, in Uganda. Vive nel Regno Unito, a Mallorca, alle Isole Canarie e in India; oltre che alla fotografia, si dedica a varie altre attività, tra le quali la gestione di un Ashtanga Yoga Shala. Nel corso di un viaggio d'affari in Asia legato alla propria attività nel settore degli arredi artigianali, si sente ispirato a creare un libro sulla cultura buddhista. Scrive quindi a Sua Santità il Dalai Lama illustrandogli il progetto e chiedendogli la sua benedizione e una lettera introduttiva che questi cortesemente gli concede. Nella primavera del 2007, Robin lascia il Regno Unito per tre mesi durante i quali si dedica intensamente alla fotografia nel Sud e nel Sud-est asiatico. Il viaggio si dimostra assai più impegnativo del previsto per il caldo e l'umidità che mettono a dura prova sia il fotografo sia la sua attrezzatura, per la durata del viaggio e per le condizioni di luce proibitive all'interno dei templi. La motivazione che spinge Robin a occuparsi di questo progetto nasce da un profondo interesse per la filosofia buddhista: "Ho pensato a quale elemento del buddhismo mi avesse attratto fin dal primo momento e credo che si tratti della compassione, della comprensione profonda del suo significato e di come essa possa essere integrata nella vita quotidiana di ognuno di noi."

page 20/21
Vietnam. Nha Trang.
Long Son Pagoda.
Nine-meter-high White Buddha.

page 23
Vietnam. Ho Chi Minh City.
Vinh Nghiem Pagoda.

page 24/25
Vietnam. Nha Trang.
Long Son Pagoda.
Reclining Buddha.

page 26
Laos. Vang Xang. Built in
the 11th century. Five
Buddha statues remain.
Allegedly, they stand on a
former elephant cemetery.

page 27
Laos. Vang Xang.
Detail of a *mudra*
carved in stone.

page 28/29
Laos. Luang Prabang.
Wat Xieng Thong.
Reclining Buddha.

page 30
Laos. Luang Prabang.
A young monk studying
English.

page 31
Laos. Luang Prabang.
Wat Visoun. Built in 1513,
it is the oldest operating
temple in Luang Prabang.

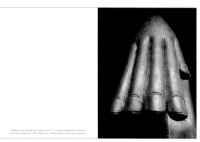

page 33
Laos. Luang Prabang. Wat Sensoukharam.
Built in 1714, it is the house of a large standing Buddha.
Detail of his hand.

page 34/35
Laos. Luang Prabang.
Wat Visoun.
"Calling For Rain Buddhas."

page 36
Laos. Luang Prabang.
Wat Nong Sikhunmeuang.
Originally built in 1729,
it burned in 1774 and
was rebuilt in 1804.

page 37
Laos. Luang Prabang.
Sitting Buddha statue.
UNESCO world heritage site.

page 38
Laos. Luang Prabang.
Wat Visoun.

page 40/41
Laos. Vientiane. Wat Sisaket.
Vientiane's oldest surviving temple,
it was restored by the French in 1924.
"Wall of Buddhas."

page 42/43
Cambodia. Kampong Trach.
Caves.

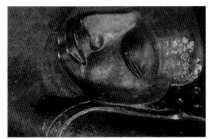

page 44/45
Cambodia. Near Angkor Wat. Phnom Kulen. Situated on
Cambodia's most sacred mountain. Reclining Buddha
carved out of the sandstone boulder at the summit

page 47
Thailand. Bangkok.
Wat Mahathat.

page 48
Thailand. Bangkok.
Wat Intharawihan.
32-meters-high and ten-meters-
wide, standing Buddha.

page 49
Thailand. Bangkok.
Wat Mahathat.

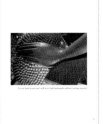

page 50
Thailand. Bangkok.
Wat Saket.

page 51
Thailand. Bangkok.
Wat Pho.

page 52
Thailand. Bangkok.
Wat Mahathat.

page 53
Thailand. Bangkok.
Wat Pho. This golden
Buddha is designed to
illustrate the passing of
the Buddha into Nirvana.

page 54/55
Thailand. Bangkok.
Wat Pho.

page 57
Thailand. Ayutthaya.
Wat Suwan Dararam.

page 58/59
Thailand. Ayutthaya. Wat Lokayasutharam.
Two monks on a pilgrimage in front of a large,
29-meters-long reclining Buddha.

page 60
Thailand. Ayutthaya.
Wat Phra Mahathat.
Built in 1384.

page 61
Thailand. Ayutthaya.
Wat Phra Mahathat. Buddha
in *Bhumisparsha Mudra*.

page 62/63
Thailand. Ayutthaya.
Wat Yai Chai Mongkol.
Built in 1357.

page 64
Thailand. Nakhon Pathom.
Phra Pathom Chedi. The
tallest Buddhist monument
in the world. The *stupa* is
125 meters high.

page 65
Thailand. Nakhon Pathom.
Phra Pathom Chedi.

page 66/67
Thailand. Sukhothai.
Wat Mahathat.
Built in 1374.

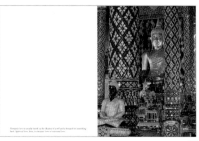

page 69
Thailand. Chiang Mai.
Wat Chama Devi.

page 70
Thailand. Chiang Mai.
Wat Phra That Doi Suthep.

page 72/73
Burma. Yangon-Bago Road. Kyaikpun Buddhas.
Four 30-meters-high seated Buddhas.

page 74
Burma. Yangon.
Shwedagon Pagoda.

page 75
Burma. Yangon.
Shwedagon Pagoda.

page 76
Burma. Bagan. Ananda Pa-
goda. West facing Buddha.

page 77
Burma. Bagan.
Dhammayangyi Pagoda.
One of a pair of Buddhas
sitting together.

page 78/79
Burma. Bagan. Sulamani Pahto.
Built in the 12th century.
Corner showing two Buddhas and old frescoes.

page 80
Burma. Bagan.
Htilominlo Pahto.

page 81
Burma. Bagan.
Htilominlo Pahto.

page 82
Burma. Bagan.
Khay Min Ga Temple.

page 83
Burma. Bagan.
Sulamani Pahto.

page 84
Burma. Bagan.

page 85
Burma. Bagan. Temple
overlooking the Ayeyarwady
River. A senior monk in
front of an ancient Buddha.

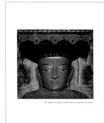

page 86
Burma. Bagan.
Sulamani Pahto.

page 87
Burma. Bagan. Sulamani
Pahto. Fine frescoes from
the Konbaung period.

page 88/89
Burma. Bagan. Shinbinthalyaung Temple (1047–1287).
A meditating monk in front of a large Parinibbana Buddha
illuminated by candlelight.

page 90
Nepal. Kathmandu.
Swayambhunath Temple
or "Monkey Temple."

page 91
Nepal. Kathmandu.
Swayambhunath Temple.
Bronze statue of Green Tara,
a female Buddha. She is
considered to be the goddess
of universal compassion.

page 92
Nepal. Kathmandu.
Swayambhunath Temple. A
group of very young monks
playing around the temple.

page 93
Nepal. Kathmandu.

page 95
Nepal. Kathmandu.
Bodhnath *Stupa* (600 AD).
"The Eyes of Bodhnath."

page 96
India. Ladakh.
Likir Gompa.

page 97
India. Ladakh. Rizong
Gompa. A senior monk at
the rooftop of a monastery.

page 99
India. Bodhgaya.
Bhutanese temple.

page 100/101
India. Ladakh. Lamayuru Gompa (10th century).
This is the oldest gompa in Ladakh.

page 102
India. Ladakh. Thiksey
Gompa. Maitreya Buddha.
"The Loving One."

page 103
India. Ladakh.
Thiksey Gompa.

page 105
India. Ladakh. Likir Gompa.
Founded in the 14th century.
A 25-meter-high Maitreya Buddha.

page 106
India. Ladakh. Namgyal
Tsemo Gompa. Prayer flags
overlooking Leh.

page 107
India. Ladakh.
View of an old village in
the Himalayan mountains.

page 108
India. Ladakh.
Thiksey Gompa.
Morning prayer.

page 110/111
Sri Lanka. Anuradhapura. Isurumuniya Vihara
(3rd century BC). A rock temple built during
the Devanampiya Tissa kingdom.

page 112/113
Sri Lanka. Dambulla. Raja Maha Vihara
(1st century BC). It contains 150 Buddha images.

page 114
Sri Lanka. Dambulla.
The Lord Buddha's feet.

page 115
Sri Lanka. Kandy.
Gadaladeniya Temple (1344).
Ancient Buddhist relic.

IMPRINT

© 2009 teNeues Verlag GmbH + Co. KG, Kempen
Photographs © 2009 Robin Kyte-Coles. All rights reserved.
www.spiritofbuddha.com

Foreword by His Holiness the Dalai Lama
Introduction, buddhist teachings by Geshe Tashi Tsering
Captions by Robin Kyte-Coles
Translations by Zoratti studio editoriale:
Ursula Varchmin (German)
Virginie de Bermond-Gettle (French)
Almudena Sassiain-Calle (Spanish)
Giulio Monteduro (Italian)
Design by Anika Leppkes
Editorial coordination by Pit Pauen
Production by Nele Jansen
Color separation by ORT, Krefeld

Published by teNeues Publishing Group

teNeues Verlag Gmbh + Co. KG
Am Selder 37, 47906 Kempen, Germany
Phone: 0049-(0)2152-916-0
Fax: 0049-(0)2152-916-111
e-mail: books@teneues.de

Press department: Andrea Rehn
Phone: 0049-(0)2152-916-202
e-mail: arehn@teneues.de

teNeues Publishing Company
16 West 22nd Street, New York, NY 10010, USA
Phone: 001-212-627-9090
Fax: 001-212-627-9511

teNeues Publishing UK Ltd.
York Villa, York Road, Byfleet, KT14 7HX, Great Britain
Phone: 0044-1932-4035-09
Fax: 0044-1932-4035-14

teNeues France S.A.R.L.
93, rue Bannier, 45000 Orléans, France
Phone: 0033-2-3854-1071
Fax: 0033-2-3862-5340

www.teneues.com

ISBN: 978-3-8327-9315-9

Printed in Italy

Bibliographic information published by the Deutsche Nationalbibliothek.
The Deutsche Nationalbibliothek lists this publication in the Deutsche Nationalbibliografie;
detailed bibliographic data are available in the Internet at http://dnb.d-nb.de.